Hurt People, Hurt People, but Healed People, Heal People

(Healing through my testimonies and God's word)

"He Heals the brokenhearted and binds up their wounds"
Psalm 147:3 (NIV)

CAPRICIA GRIFFIN

DEDICATION

This book is dedicated to me: I've faced countless challenges in my life that most people wouldn't believe if I hadn't written this. I'm incredibly proud of the courage and confidence it took to share my story through my testimonies, and for the healing it may bring to others. A well-deserved salute to myself!

I'd also like to dedicate this book to my late uncle, Jerome: You were one of my greatest supporters. I'm so thankful I had the chance to share my blog posts with you. You always bragged about me to everyone, proudly telling them how much you believed in me. You expressed how happy you were that I was finally sharing my story and stepping into my purpose. I love you, Uncle, and the memories we shared will always remain in my heart.

TABLE OF CONTENTS

Acknowledgments...05
Chapter 1...07
Chapter 2...10
Chapter 3...14
Chapter 4...18
Chapter 5...23
Chapter 6...28
Chapter 7...35
Chapter 8...40
Chapter 9...46
Chapter 10...52
Chapter 11...59
Chapter 12...64
Chapter 13...73
Chapter 14...83
Chapter 15...90
Chapter 16...98
Chapter 17...105
Chapter 18...112
Chapter 19...120
Chapter 20...127
Chapter 21...134
Chapter 22...140

Acknowledgments

But first and foremost, let me THANK GOD : God, I couldn't have done this without you. You gave me this vision as a child, but it wasn't until I sought you daily that you gave me the courage, confidence, and faith to know anything is possible with you.

To My husband, Quindell: Thank you for being the man God created you to be. Your love, support, and belief in me made it easier to create this book. I couldn't have asked for a better partner.

I'm deeply grateful to my parents, Elaine and Willie: Thank you both for always believing in me and supporting my choices. I'm grateful for the freedom to speak my truth, regardless of others' opinions. Thank you for teaching me about God, helping me distinguish between the spirit and the flesh, and guiding me to follow His vision when it was time to write it.

Acknowledgments (Cont.)

To My Kids: Thank you for your love, support, and for promoting my work. It means the world to me that you share my material and believe in me. I'm grateful to show you that with God's help, all things are possible.

To My sister, Regina, and nephew Arrentheny: Thank you, Sis, for editing my work with so much care. It means a lot knowing it was in the right hands. I'm grateful for your generosity and thoughtfulness. Thank you, Nephew, for encouraging me to leap out on faith and "Do it Afraid."

Thank you to all my best friends, my extended family, and blog post subscribers: I couldn't have done it without you all. Thank you for your support and loyalty—you inspire me to keep pushing forward, no matter the obstacles.

Chapter 1

STOP LISTENING TO SOCIETY

Most of us are not truly happy within ourselves because we have let society tell us lies about ourselves and what we should be doing in our lives. We can't please everyone so why try? You will never be happy if you are always worried about what others think about you and if you start your life around what others tell you then you will never truly be happy and successful. One thing I learned is the Pharisees and scribes talked about Jesus so of course people are going to talk about us because Jesus was perfect and we're far from perfect. You have to realize that people who talk about you aren't happy with themselves. No matter what you do, someone will always have something negative to say. If you're a big-boned or heavy-set person some people close to you will say you are too big and need to lose weight and then if you lose the weight or if you're a skinny person. The people close to you will tell you that you need meat on your bones and no man or woman wants a toothpick but who are they to tell you what you need to do with your body? Stop letting people rush you to make decisions that may affect you later in your life. At the end of the day whatever decision you make you have to live with those decisions, not others. I know a lot of people feel like once they get a certain age something is wrong with them if they haven't got married, had a child, or maybe aren't further in life than they thought they would be. We feel that way because society has told us that we have to be married by a certain age or something must be wrong with us or if we don't have a child we can't have kids and none of that is true. Your clock is not running out just because society says it is. Some people get married in their 90s and even have children in their 40s and are still happy and they didn't rush because they felt like their clock was ticking. You let God direct your paths and stop making decisions off what society has told you.

But the LORD said to Samuel, *"Do not consider his appearance or his height, for I have rejected him. The LORD does not look at the things man looks at. Man looks at the outward appearance, but the LORD looks at the heart."* ~ **1 Samuel 16:7**

Chapter 2

HEALING PROCESS/ DON'T GIVE THEM YOUR POWER

I'm 41 years old and I'm just starting to truly heal and step into my purpose. The reason I'm mentioning my age is because so many women and men feel like they should be healed from past things that have hurt them and that's not always the case. I know that some people in your circle may look at you crazy because you are still mourning over things that hurt you or maybe a pet that passed away but no one can tell you how long it takes to heal from things. We are all different and heal at different times. So, remember healing doesn't have a deadline. There are people in their 50s and 60s still trying to heal from things they went through in their childhood so trust me when I say you're not alone. I have tried so many things to try and speed up my healing process. I would fast and pray, read devotions, listen to sermons and podcasts, go to church, etc and I still wasn't healing the way I thought I should be, and guess what that is okay. In my opinion, the healing doesn't start until you take accountability for your part in certain situations or Let Go and Let God handle certain people who did you wrong even though you may not deserve what they did to you. I know that's easier said than done but you have to. **Ephesians 4:32 says "Be kind to one another, tenderhearted, forgiving one another, as God in Christ forgave you."** I know it's hard to forgive some people but you have to forgive to heal. That doesn't mean you have to allow them back in your life but you do have to forgive so that you can heal because if not you will allow the pain to consume you. There have been plenty of times when I thought I was truly healed only to find out I wasn't healed at all. If you're still crying when you talk about certain things or people who hurt you then you're not completely healed.

If you feel your spirit getting angry at the sound of someone's voice or their name mentioned because you dislike that person then you aren't completely healed. If it triggers your spirit when you see that person face to face then you're not healed. If you feel the need to always defend yourself then you aren't healed. That was one of my weaknesses. I felt the need to always defend myself when people lied on me or if someone tried to throw shade my way. I felt like I had to respond because I refused to let them spread lies about me or think they punked me, so I would always respond. I had to learn that all I was doing was giving them power over me and falling into the devil's plan to upset me. The devil always comes to steal, kill, and destroy so you always have to be alert. What I learned is that I don't need to always respond because God will fight my battles for me and being silent is a response. My sister Regina shared a quote by Eleanor Roosevelt that helped me with my healing process so I'm going to share that quote with you as well. **" No one can make you feel inferior without your consent" "NEVER GIVE IT!"** That's what they want you to do. When you respond to a toxic person you just give them power over you. Remember, they are miserable and misery loves company so don't join their party. Trust me when I tell you they purposely wanted to upset you and by responding you let them know that they got under your skin and that's when you gave them your power. I know some people can say some mean and hateful things and even do some evil things but no matter what they say or do give it to God because he can handle them more than we can. **"But remember that they will have to face God, who stands ready to judge everyone, both the living and the dead" ~1 Peter 4:5~**

Chapter 3

DISTRACTIONS THAT KEEP YOU

FROM THE WORD

I believe that most of us get off course because we are always distracted by things and people, and that keeps us from growing in our lives. I've talked to so many people who say they don't read their Bible because they don't have time but that's not true. A lot of times we don't read our Bible because we get distracted by other things and people. You make time for what is important to you. That's the trick of the enemy. He knows that if he distracts us we won't read the word and the word is what we need to plant in our hearts for us to succeed in this life. We have to remember that life is a journey and by reading the word that is how God keeps breathing new life in our spirit daily. *Matthew 4:4 says " Man shall not live on bread alone, but on every word that proceeds out through the mouth of God.* " Have you noticed every time you start to read your Bible you get sleepy all of a sudden? That happens because that is the enemy trying to distract you from reading the word. He knows that if you're sleepy you won't always attain what you are reading in the Bible. That's why we have to make time for God and give him the same attention we would give our husband/boyfriend, our children, our parents, and our friends. If you're alert then you will understand everything that you are reading and if you don't understand it then pray and ask God to help you understand what you are reading so that you can apply it to your life daily. Sometimes you can be in church and all of a sudden you start thinking about what chores you need to do once you get home like cooking, washing clothes and dishes, etc. That happens because it's something that the pastor is saying that you need to hear and the devil doesn't want you to get that word inside of you because he knows that the word is our lamp unto our feet and the light unto our path. When that happens change your mindset and get back focus so that you can hear what God is trying to say to you through the pastor that you are listening to. Think about how you may be about to get ready to read your bible or you have been thinking about picking up your Bible to read and then all of a sudden a friend or family member calls you and then you end up talking to them on the phone for hours or you decide to leave the house and meet them somewhere once again that was satan's way of distracting you so that you forget to read your Bible. If you think about reading your Bible immediately, put your phone on, do not disturb, follow your spirit, and read the word. More likely your spirit was guiding you to read the word for a reason so don't let the enemy distract you and keep you from reading your Bible. The same goes for social media. If you plan on reading your Bible don't even glance at social media because as soon as you open up that app you immediately will become distracted by posts, reels, etc so don't do it. God is jealous of our heart and he wants us to give him our undivided attention just like we give others. If you want to succeed in life you have to figure out how to put God first in everything you do, put God first and he will direct you and crown your efforts with success. If you don't read the word you are going to continue to get distracted and listen to the enemy lies that he tells us to keep us from growing. Don't let the enemy win with the battlefield of the mind because you have control over your life so you can stop the distractions but only if you put your mind to it and stay alert. ~ *Be self Controlled and alert your enemy the devil prowls around like a roaring lion looking for someone to devour, resist* **him standing firm in the faith" 1 Peter 5:8**

Chapter 4

DO IT AFRAID

One thing I have learned is that we have to just do things we are afraid of. I realized that I have had so many dreams and goals but I never started them or I began but stopped out of fear. Just like now I started this blog and have several other things I want to start and I'm afraid but I refuse to let my fear stop me from my goals and what God put in my spirit to accomplish. I had to ask myself this question and I want you to do the same. What is the worst thing that could happen? Once we get past that I think we can move forward. *"And the LORD answered me: "Write the vision; make it plain on tablets, so he may run who reads it. For still the vision awaits its appointed time; it hastens to the end—it will*

not lie. If it seems slow, wait for it; it will surely come; it will not delay." ~Habakkuk 2:2~ For you to get started with whatever goal you have for yourself or whatever your heart desires you have to first write down your vision and make it plain like the bible verse says. Then write down the steps you plan on taking to bring that vision to fruition. Once you write down the steps, ask yourself what things may go wrong. If it does, what steps will I take to make sure I don't stop due to fear? When things go wrong, which sometimes they will, we have to learn to keep going and not let those setbacks stop us from what we started or what we hope to start because we are afraid of the results. Even if no one is rooting or cheering you on, don't let that stop you from doing whatever your goal is. Some people will even try to talk you out of your plans but don't let them. God put the vision in your spirit not theirs so they may not understand what God has chosen you to do and that's okay they don't have to. If you start feeling afraid, change your mindset because that's only Satan trying to stop you from what God has put in your spirit to do. *"For God has not given us a spirit of fear, but of power and love and of a sound mind" ~ 2 Timothy 1:7~* We have to realize that God wouldn't have given us this vision if he wasn't going to help us bring it to pass. We have to learn to get out of our comfort zone and out of our own way. A lot of times we psych ourselves out and then we quit and it's all because of fear. We all could accomplish so many things, and we still can if we just Do It Afraid. If things fall apart that's fine just start over. Every famous person had to go through trials and tribulations before they got to where they are and that is the same for us but with God on our side *" We can do all things through Christ who gives us strength" ~Philippians 4:13~* Remember no matter what it is that you want to do, do it afraid. If you want to go to a movie at the movie theater but you don't have anyone to go with you then go by yourself. I know several people who said they have never been to a movie or out to eat by themselves due to what other people may think. Who cares what they think, do not be afraid and go enjoy that movie and enjoy a quiet lunch or dinner in peace by yourself. You may want to try a new hobby like sewing or playing tennis but you're afraid that you won't catch on quickly so you think about quitting. Do it afraid and watch how you enjoy it. Doing it afraid means with anything you do in life no matter what it is. If you want to go see your favorite artist at a concert but you don't have anyone to go with you then purchase your ticket and go by yourself even if you're afraid. Trust me once you get there you will not feel like you're by yourself so do it afraid and watch how you enjoy yourself once you let the fear roll off your back. If there is a position at your job you want to apply for but you're afraid you will never get that position because you believe that you don't qualify for the position. Do It Afraid. The worst thing that could happen is you don't get the position and if you don't that's okay because that just means God has something better in store for you or it may just not be your time yet. If you ever feel that way I want you to always remember that God doesn't call the qualified. He qualifies the called. Stop being afraid of what could go wrong and think about what could go right. *"When I am afraid, I put my trust in You. In God, whose word I* **praise in God I trust. I will not be afraid. What can man do to me"** ~Psalm 56: 3-4~

Chapter 5

STOP BEING SO INSENSITIVE

I feel like there are so many insensitive people in this world and it's sad. A lot of people feel like just because they know you they can say anything even if it's insensitive. Some people may not even realize certain things they ask are insensitive so I'm going to speak on some insensitive things in this post. It is very insensitive when you ask a female when she is going to have a child or have another child. For one, you have no idea if that female can even have kids and that may be something that she is struggling with and now you brought that up and triggered her spirit and messed up her day. I remember two different family members asked me questions regarding having another child. The first person asked me when I was going to have another child so that my son wouldn't be the only child even though he had step-siblings. The second family member had the nerve to tell me that I needed to have a child with my husband or I would regret not having one since he had kids with other women already. Which was very insensitive to me. I had just lost twins in 2017 due to an ectopic pregnancy loss which they were aware of. I wouldn't wish that pain on anyone. I was just starting to heal when that person brought that back up not knowing my husband and I both had agreed we no longer wanted to have any more kids and risk going through that pain again. So, please be careful what you ask a person because you never know if that is a sensitive topic or not for that individual. *"Be kind to everyone. Be Patient with difficult people" 2 Timothy 2:24* Stop Asking people when they are going to get married. Whether that person gets married or not it's none of your business. How do you know if that person even wants to get married? That person may have gone through a bad divorce and never wants to get married again yet you act like their decision is wrong because you feel like they need to be married. Marriage is not for everyone so I wish people would stop trying to push that topic on other people. The person you're talking to may want to get married but keeps dating the wrong person and now you bring up the marriage topic and make them feel bad and that's exactly what happens when some people jump into wrong relationships just because they want to please others so they marry someone unequally yoked. *"Show respect to Everyone" 1 Peter 2:17* Another very insensitive thing is when someone loses a family member and you put their personal business on social media before the immediate family can tell you about their own family business. No one wants to get on social media and see things like that especially when they are close to that person. I remember having an anxiety attack at work while on a phone call with a patient because on my break I chose to go on Facebook and that's when I saw that my aunt had passed away and I hadn't even received the phone call yet. I remember looking at my aunt's kid's pages and not even one of them had posted about it yet but another family member chose to post about it. Put yourself in their shoes and think before you post something insensitive to others. ***"Do to others as you would have them do to you" Luke 6:31*** Sometimes family members or friends may fall out with each other for some time. It is very insensitive when others try to get in the middle of a situation that has nothing to do with them. If two family members or friends are at odds with each other, mind your business and stop being insensitive and pressuring them to talk to one another. You have no idea what that person may have gone through during that altercation so you need to stay out of it. We love to try to force one another to get over things that hurt them and that's why so many people never heal because they sweep things under the rug. When those family members/friends are ready to talk they will on their own time. Just because you feel like they need to be speaking with one another doesn't mean that's what needs to be done. We have to learn to set boundaries with one another so that certain lines aren't crossed and other people need to butt out. If they choose not to work it out. It is not your place to tell them they should. **"And let us consider how to stir up one another to love and good works" Hebrews 10:24**

Chapter 6

CHALLENGES OF A BLENDED FAMILY

I could write a whole book on this topic which maybe one day I just might. "I was thrown so much in the past, but things have been getting better since my husband and I chose to let God fight this battle. We gave up the need to try and take control of the situation with all parties involved."I wasn't sure what to write about because I have so many stories I could tell you all about when it comes to being in a blended family. I will write about a few incidents that I went through and I pray that my testimony will help someone else who may be struggling in a blended family. When you are in a blended family just know that things aren't always going to be peachy all the time especially when you have to deal with another person that isn't happy within themselves. When my husband and I first got married that's when all the drama started. When two of my step-kids came to our house. We were told days before that we needed to buy clothes and hygiene products for them because their mother refused to pack those items for the kids to bring with them. I just couldn't believe that someone would be so hateful especially when it comes to your kids. I put myself in her shoes and I still couldn't see myself ever being that hateful to my son's father so I just told my husband we would go buy them whatever they needed because, at the end of the day, it's not the kid's fault. My husband wanted to go off on his kid's mother at that time and he had absolutely every right to feel that way but like I told him misery loves company and it doesn't live over here so we will continue to go high when she goes low and that's something we still live by today and I'm telling you to also do the same.

"Vengeance is mine, I will repay, says the Lord" Romans 12:19

One night, I remember telling all the kids to go to bed, but my step-kids decided that they didn't have to listen to me so when my son got in his bed they decided to call their mom and talk on the phone. I remember, my son complaining to me telling me that it wasn't fair that he had to go to bed but they didn't and not only that when it was time to go to bed my son came in the room and told my husband and I both good night but when it came to my step-kids they came in the room and told my husband good night and acted like I didn't exist. That hurt me so bad because I had never in my life been mistreated by a child before and It wasn't fair that all the kids were given rules to follow but only my son followed those rules. I remember going to my mother's house that night and I cried in her arms and told her that I didn't think I would be able to do it because I wouldn't be disrespected in my own home and my husband acted like it wasn't a problem at all. That night my mother had a long talk with my husband and me about how the enemy was trying to come between us and that we didn't need to let him win. The next day my husband

talked with his kids and he told them that all rules applied to them

as well and he started taking up their phone at bedtime. He even

talked with their mom and let her know that we had rules at our

house and they had to follow them just like my son did. So, if

you've been through this just know you aren't alone but things do

get better in due time. *"Lord, you have heard the desires of* **the**

humble. You will prepare their hearts. You will cause your ear

to hear," ~Psalms 10:17~ One of the main things that I know a lot

of blended families go through is that the non-custodial parent is

not able to see the kids like they want to, and that is no different

for our family. My husband and I got married in 2020, but weren't

able to have all the kids at our wedding due to him not seeing his

kids in over a year because of his kid's mother being spiteful

because he had moved on in a relationship with me and she was

jealous. There were days when she would

call and ask my husband to pick up the kids and then he would drive 3 hours there just for her to be funny and say she would not let him get them until my husband said enough was enough and he took her to court for visitation and even after that we still had some problems. Some days she didn't want to meet us to get the kids or some days we had the kids and we had to drive them back the whole way because she would make up excuses of why she couldn't meet us halfway or she would just come out and say you can drive the whole way because I don't feel like driving down the road. The police were called several times due to the visitation agreement being violated on the custodial parent's end until my husband and I got to the point where we just stopped going back and forth with her because we knew that's what she wanted him to do. If you are happy in your relationship or marriage please don't let the other parent come between you because that is the devil's plan. He purposely wants to split you up so if he can call a division in your home then he will. My husband and I continue to stay in prayer together. We refuse to let the mess consume us too. **"God will repay each person according to his works" ~Romans 2:6~** I know that it's hurtful but most of the time the custodial parent will even bad mouth you and your significant other to the kids so that energy will reciprocate when the kids are around the non-custodial parent and their partner. So many lies and mean things have been told about my husband and myself. My husband has even received a video with one of his kids saying they hate him and how ugly his little girlfriend was referring to me at that time. This video was sent in the beginning stages of my husband and I's relationship when the kids were a lot younger. Guess why that happened? It happened because the other parent was hurt so she wanted to hurt my husband. I've been saying it all along hurt people, hurt people and that's what this is all about. That video brought sadness to my eyes because I hated seeing a broken person use her kids to hurt another individual not knowing how much damage that is causing our kids. I realized then that she was damaged and lashing out at us and that there was nothing that we could ever do or say to her to change how she felt because she was scorned. I vowed to not return the favor and show all my kids how adults should act and handle conflict and that's what I'm going to continue to do. I'm a healed person so I plan on spreading light by healing others instead of paying evil for evil. What I learned is that arguing with a fool makes you just as foolish.

"Fools have no interest in understanding, they only want to air their own opinion" Proverbs 18:2 (NLT)

Chapter 7

DO YOU TRUST GOD?

When your back is against the wall do you truly trust God? Most of us say that we truly trust God and we profess how much love we have for Jesus and God all the time. We even quote bible verses like *"I can do all things through Christ who strengthens me"* *~Philippians 4:13~*but the true test of how much we trust God is how we respond when things in our life aren't going well. The devil is constantly testing us daily and he wants us to curse God and not believe in him at all. The way Job was tested, some of us will be tested just like that, but the question is when that happens will you trust God to fight your battle for you or will you fall for the devil's scheme and let your emotions control your behavior? **In Job 2:9 His wife said to him, "Are you still maintaining your integrity? Curse God and die!"** Thank goodness Job didn't listen to his wife when she told him that because if he had then he would have missed out on his blessing and he would have let the devil's plan come to fruition, but God knew that Job loved him and he already knew that Job would pass the test. Just like, God blessed Job with double he will also do the same for us if we put all our trust in him not just some of it. Most of the time we don't truly trust God and that's why we keep having the same tests but just in different ways. *We say we live by Faith but not by Sight ~2 Corinthians 5:7~* but as soon as something that is out of our control happens we lose it. My faith is being tested daily but especially even more now, I realized since I started this blog website my faith has been tested even more, but I'm not surprised at all because Satan doesn't like it when we are spreading the word and trying to help others and he wants us to stay stuck. I was hit from behind on the day after my birthday which was Christmas Eve on my way back from Georgia to North Carolina in 2023. My car was still drivable so I drove it back home. I went to several shops in my city and not far from me only to be told that they couldn't work on my truck until April or May 2024. My traction light and other signals came up on my dashboard so I knew that I couldn't wait that long to have my truck looked at. I finally found a shop an hour away that said they could take it but that wasn't until the middle of January 2024. My truck was towed and I was happy to know that it would be fixed but I found out that my truck was considered a total loss. The worth of my truck exceeded what I owed the lender because I lacked gap insurance. Following the total loss of my truck, my husband started experiencing car problems post-expensive repairs totaling over $1,000. I could get angry, complain, and ask God why things are always happening to me, but I'm not. If I do, I don't trust God completely and I'm not living by Faith and I'm living by Sight. So, when I say Do you trust God? I'm asking you, can you give up the control to fix everything? *"Be Still. Let Go and Let God" ~Psalm 46:10~* So many of us have lost family members due to COVID-19, medical conditions, suicide, or even domestic violence and we don't understand why God allowed us to lose those family members. When you lose a family member or multiple people in your family all at once sometimes you question God and your Faith waivers. These are the times when we must stay in prayer and seek God for strength and guidance. Try your best not to question God. He doesn't make any mistakes even though we may not understand why he has taken that person out of our lives. So I ask again, do you completely trust God? Trust me I used to question God about everything and that's what made me realize that I didn't completely trust him the way I was supposed to. *"Jesus replied, " You don't understand now what I am doing, but someday you will" ~ John 13:7~* Most of us have been heartbroken by a person that we fell in love with or heartbroken by a person that we trusted. We would have given this person the clothes off our back if they needed them yet that's the same person who broke us. Sometimes this happens with several people that we have trusted in our life. It's hard to understand why someone so close to us would hurt us that way. We start questioning God again, on why he allowed us to continually get our hearts broken and sometimes we react out of anger and try to do things out of revenge instead of trusting God to handle that person who hurt us. When you let go of the need to try and fix the problem or you take it upon yourself to punish that person, that's when you can say you completely trust God. **" *The Lord* is close to the broken-hearted and saves those who are crushed in spirit." ~ Psalm 34:18~**

Chapter 8

FORGIVENESS

What is the meaning of Forgiveness? According to The Greater Good Science Center at the University of California, Berkeley **Forgiveness is a conscious, deliberate decision to release feelings of resentment or vengeance toward a person or group who has harmed you, regardless of whether they deserve your forgiveness.** I realized forgiveness is one of the hardest things for people to do. I believe that it's hard to forgive because we often feel like the person who wronged us needs to be held accountable for their actions and we feel like if we forgive that person so quickly they will never learn from their mistakes and now that you've been hurt by that person the trust has been broken. We must learn that forgiving others isn't about them. It's about yourself and making sure you have a pure heart and clear mind no matter what the next person has done. This is a part of the Devil's plan. He likes for us to harbor unforgiveness in our hearts so that our hearts become hardened. God wants us to have a pure heart. *Matthew 5:8 says " Blessed are the pure in heart, for they shall see God."* I have experienced mistreatment from many people, leading me to develop a hardened heart towards some of them at times. I had to realize that everything happens for a reason and that I could either let this person have power over me or I could forgive them and take my power back. Just because you forgive a person doesn't mean you have to allow them back into your life. You can also love them from a distance. Forgiveness doesn't mean you forget but it means you won't bring it up again. Also, just because you forgive them doesn't mean you have to have a conversation with them and tell them that you forgave them. All you have to do is have a conversation with God and repent. *" Love prospers when a fault is forgiven, but dwelling on it separates close friends" ~Proverbs 17:9~* I know

some of you may say, well, you don't know what that person has

done to me and that person is someone that it's hard to forgive.

Trust me I get it. I have become so mad at a person that I wished

death on them and I knew that was wrong but that's how bad that

person hurt me that I felt like they didn't deserve to be on this

Earth. I even questioned why God allowed horrible people to live

but allowed amazing people to leave this Earth so soon. It was so

hard to forgive those people who made me feel that way about

them because of how badly they hurt me and it was hard for me to

forgive God at times. I was scorned. Holding a grudge towards

someone can make you very bitter and even raise your blood

pressure. I knew that forgiving them was something that I needed

to do for myself. I wanted peace and I didn't want my spirit to be

disturbed anymore when I was around that individual or if I heard

something about them that was negative. Take

forgiveness slowly, don't blame yourself for being slow to forgive

if it's hard for you right now. Peace will come.

Forgive those who hurt you, but never forget what it taught you.

When you choose to forgive those who have hurt you, you take

away their power. *"Remember, the Lord forgave you, so you must*

forgive others. " ~ Colossians 3:13~ (NLT) We also must learn to

forgive ourselves for not knowing what we didn't know before we

learned it. God forgives us so we know how to learn how to

forgive ourselves. Often, we question ourselves on why we made

certain choices after things didn't turn out the way we wished.

Sometimes, it's hard for us to forgive ourselves because we have

made the same mistakes repeatedly. We don't understand why we

continue to make the same mistakes. It's okay you will eventually

be strong and wise enough to forgive yourself and you will get

over that situation that is holding you back. Even if someone keeps

blaming you for something that happened to you or

something that you may have done. Forgive yourself and move forward. You're still here to fight another day and tell your story. If you need to repent and keep it moving. A lot of times when we don't forgive ourselves we build walls and walls not only keep people out it keeps us locked in. We can't grow if we don't learn to forgive ourselves just as we forgive others. We are all human and we all make mistakes. That's why Jesus died on the cross for us because God already knew we would sin on this Earth and he has already forgiven us for it. The moment you ask God to forgive you is the moment you need to leave the guilt behind. *Psalms 32:5 " I acknowledged my mistakes to you and you forgave them"* Learning to forgive ourselves for things that were out of our control is something else we must work on. We stay stuck a lot of times and blame ourselves for things that happened to us that we had no control over. We feel like it's something we could have done better if we had just thought about it at that moment or regret that we didn't do anything at all afterward out of fear. Or, it could be we know we had no control over what happened to us but someone else blames us for what happened. I don't care what the situation was, if you had no control over it, don't blame yourself, and don't allow anyone to make you feel ashamed for something that happened to you. Forgive yourself for believing things about yourself that aren't true and never have been true. *" We all fall short of the glory of God" ~ Romans 3:23~*

Chapter 9

BE CAREFUL WHAT YOU CONSUME

We must start being careful what we let inside our brains because it easily affects our attitude. A lot of people don't believe it but the battle is in the mind. That's why a lot of people are moody. Have you ever noticed that one minute you will be thinking about positive things and then later you start thinking about negative things? More than likely it was because of whatever you let inside your brain. I'm going to tell you some things that I believe we need to be careful about consuming. We need to be careful what we are watching on television or at the movie theater. Everything that we watch is just a seed being planted in our brains. That's why if you watch a scary movie you may have a nightmare when you fall asleep. It's because you watched something terrifying before you fell asleep and now your brain has consumed that. A lot of people have trust issues already and in my opinion, people who have trust issues shouldn't watch shows that are showing infidelity, but those are some of people's favorite shows to watch. I felt like the spirit told me a long time ago that I needed to be careful what I watch on television but I kept ignoring it. I remember reading the book "**A Battlefield of the Mind" By Joyce Meyer.** This is still one of my favorite books. In the book, Joyce Meyer talks about how we are always fighting the battle in the mind and that's what led me to start monitoring what I was watching and noticing how I was feeling after I watched shows. What I noticed was if I watched shows that showed someone committing adultery/ infidelity then afterward I would start having negative thoughts. If the person I was dating came home a few minutes later than normal I would start assuming they were out cheating, but the only reason I had those thoughts was because I had just watched a show about a person getting lied to and cheated on right before they came home. I also noticed that If I watched romantic shows I would always be in the mood to do something romantic for my significant other and that's when I knew that it was true what you consume does affect your mood if you allow it. *"Be careful what you think, because your thoughts run your life." ~ Proverbs 4:23~* Also, be careful what you're listening to, for example, podcasts, the music you stream, music on the radio, and even the news. Whatever you listen to affects your mood. If you just had a breakup don't listen to music about someone getting their heart broken because that only makes you even sadder. Why do that to yourself? You should be listening to more uplifting songs. I feel like a lot of the time we want to feel sorry for ourselves and that's why we listen to those types of songs when we're already sad. I remember in my younger years I would listen to songs like "Knuck if You Buck" By Crime Mob and "Head Bussa" By Lil Scrappy right before I would go to the club and I noticed that it would put me in a fighting mood spirit and I would be saying to myself "Nobody better try me today or it's on" and then when I would go to the club with my friends I noticed when they played those same or similar songs in the club I would be in a fight mode spirit especially when I saw a hater watching me. The only reason I was feeling like that was because of what I was consuming in my ear. I know this to also be true because I noticed that when I would listen to gospel music I would be in good spirits and when I put on that armor of God I allowed nothing to upset me. I could see the same haters on the street right after listening to gospel music and when a negative thought tried to come up I would just quote a scripture like *" Father forgive them, for they know not what they do" ~Luke 23:34~* Lastly, be careful who you let in your ear. All of us confide in at least one person about certain things that we go through, and there's nothing wrong with that. Make sure whoever you confide in is a person who is mature enough to give you wisdom and not give you advice off on their emotions, and a person who you can truly trust. We all know which person we can talk to and they are going to keep it real with us and we also know which person to call who is only going to agree with whatever you say. The person who will tell you whatever you want to hear is the person who you don't need to let in your ear. I'm going to give you an example. I just got into a heated argument with an individual over the phone. I'm now ready to fight them because something they said to me triggered my spirit. I called my sister over the phone and I told her what happened. I know that my sister is going to want every detail of what was said on that phone call and then she is going to tell me if I was right or wrong. She's also going to say something to me along the lines of that person isn't worth getting in trouble over. Just because they don't have anything to lose doesn't mean you don't. Now, if I had called someone that I'm starting to become friends with and told them what happened that person just might say something along the lines of "Girl I don't blame you and you have every right to go upside their head. If you need me let me know and I'll pull up" That's the exact type of person I'm talking about you shouldn't let in your ear. Everybody doesn't have your best interest at heart so be careful who you let in your ear and give you advice. A lot of relationships have ended because you let the wrong person in your ear tell you something about your partner which was a lie and now you're single and they are probably living their best life. Sometimes a person will give you bad advice on the person just because they are envious of you and you don't even know it and they just might be attracted to the person you're in a relationship with, so once again I tell you to be careful who you let in your ear.

" Consider carefully what you hear" ~ Mark 4:24~

Chapter 10

MARRIAGE IS NOT JUST A PIECE OF PAPER

So many people take marriage for granted. I dislike hearing people say that marriage is just a piece of paper because that isn't true. When you get married you are saying your vows before God and making a promise to God in front of your loved ones. You sign a marriage certificate because that is what the Bible calls your covenant. **"And the two will become one flesh. So they are no longer two, but one flesh" ~ Mark 10:8~** Marriage is beautiful, but it's not always easy. There are days when you feel like you want to walk away from your marriage but remember the reason you got married in the first place. Marriages may fail when individuals marry for the wrong reasons or rush into it without being a match chosen by God. It's important to carefully choose a life partner rather than settling for the first person available to avoid a doomed marriage. If God puts you together then it is both party's responsibility to put in the work to make the marriage work. I'm going to write about some things that I feel you must have to have to make the marriage work. Some of these are things that I had to learn along the way in my marriage *"And let us consider how to stir up one another to love and good works" ~ Hebrews 10:24~ Communication and Active listening* is one of the most important keys in a marriage. If you're not able to communicate effectively your marriage will continue to suffer. You also have to actively listen when you communicate. This is one of the hardest things to do sometimes because a lot of the time we listen to respond and we're already in defense mode so no matter what the person you are communicating with says you take it the wrong way. Do not hit below the belt no matter how mad you get. Never say something that you will regret later

because once you say it out of your mouth you can't take those words back. If you struggle with active listening in your relationship, try to do some active listening role-playing twice a week. If you go to **verywellmind.com** it has some great tips on how to actively listen to your partner. One is by being fully present in the conversation, showing interest by practicing good eye contact, making sure you ask open-ended questions to encourage further responses if you don't understand and withholding judgment and advice. Remember, your spouse is not a mind reader, so you have **to be honest with them about** how you feel because if you don't they have no idea you feel that way. Also, pray with your spouse even if it's once a week. *" Be completely humble and gentle, be patient, bearing with one another in love" ~ Ephesians 4:2~* When you are married you must learn to *put your spouse above yourself.* We get so used to doing whatever we want and saying whatever we want but once you get married all of that is supposed to stop. For example, before I met my husband there were certain outfits that I would wear that were revealing but now that I have a husband I ask my husband what he thinks about certain outfits before I wear them out because I never want to disrespect him and I never want him to feel like I'm showing off what belongs to him to the world. You must let go of that attitude that I'm grown, and I can wear whatever I want because if you feel that way then you will not be married long. That shows you have no respect for how your mate feels. Another example is if your spouse feels like you're hanging out with your friends more than you are home then that's a problem and you need to put your spouse's feelings first and sit down and come up with a compromise. Even if your spouse doesn't want to attend church with you, don't pressure them to do something they don't want to do.

You can be honest with them and tell them how it makes you feel that they want to go with you, but more than anything just pray and continue to go to church and watch how things change in your household *"Be devoted to one another in love. Honor one another above yourselves." ~ Romans 12:10~ Keep your friends and family out of your marriage.* I understand that everyone needs someone to talk to and that is fine. Make sure whoever you choose to talk to is a person that you can trust and you know that your business will stay between just the two of you. I also don't think it's wise to get advice from a single person unless that person has been married before. First, always go to God and you should always communicate with your spouse but sometimes I know it's just too difficult to communicate with your spouse when they are upset with you. Don't just go around calling and talking to every person you know about your spouse because that makes your spouse look bad. You have to remember once you forgive your spouse, your family and friends may have a grudge against them because of what you told them about your partner, so it's best to just keep them out of your business sometimes. ***Support your spouse*** no matter what. Sometimes it's hard to support your spouse when you don't agree with their choices. Just because your spouse doesn't make the same decisions you make doesn't mean it's not a good decision. My husband was working a job that was over an hour away from our house and I didn't like it at all. I observed that the long commute was wearing him out, and the unpredictable hours at work were causing concern, but my husband wanted to stay at this job due to the salary. I learned to support him because it became an argument at home and the last thing I want to do is have my husband be defeated at work and then come home to me complaining. Be your spouse peace when you're able to be. I started just praying about it to God and guess what my husband made the decision on his own to get another job and then he quit that long-distance job, so it worked out in the end but I had to be still and let God do the work for me. *Make sure you schedule a date night* with your spouse. It can be just the two of you or with other couples but make sure you get out of the house and spend time together. Many individuals prioritize having kids over their spouses. Your spouse should come before everyone including your kids. God is the only one that should come before your spouse. You don't have to spend money all the time either. You can just plan a movie or game night at home if you make time for each other. Don't get so busy with life that you forget about the person that you fell in love with, and you made a vow to build a foundation with.

Chapter 11

ADDICTION

What is **Addiction**? According to Healthdirect on Google

Addiction is when you have a strong physical or psychological

need or urge to do something or use something. You can be

addicted to so many things and most of us know someone who is

addicted to something or it could be ourselves who may be

addicted to something. I'm going to talk about drug and alcohol

addiction since that's what I'm most familiar with. In recent years,

most addictions have been related to drugs, alcohol, or both. I'm

sure many of us have a friend or family member struggling with

addiction. In the beginning, addiction is often overlooked, and

individuals struggling with addiction may deny its presence. I've

seen what alcohol and drugs have done to some of my loved ones

and it breaks my heart. No matter how much you tell a person who has an addiction that their addiction bothers you it won't matter unless they are ready to change on their own. I learned that some of my loved ones with addictions turn to alcohol or drugs to numb their emotional pain. They have experienced childhood trauma, bullying, domestic violence, betrayal, or lost a loved one, resulting in unresolved emotional distress. When people face pain, they often resort to alcohol or drugs to handle life's difficulties. Yet, they might not be dealing with life's challenges as effectively as they think. On the contrary, when they consume alcohol, they may display violent behavior toward those who care for them or sometimes express hurtful and unkind words towards them. Sometimes it gets to the point where family and friends no longer want to be around that individual because of their behavior when they are under the influence. No matter how bad the person with the addiction behaves please do not give up on them. Consistently keep them in your prayers, even if you must maintain a distance in your love for them. Many individuals struggling with drug addiction may resort to stealing from and deceiving their loved ones to satisfy their cravings, which can evoke feelings of anger and the urge to retaliate. Regardless of their actions, it's important to forgive them and refrain from any physical harm. If you are addicted to drugs or alcohol or it's your loved one and you don't know where to turn help is always available if you dial 988 which is the Suicide and Crisis lifeline. **"And be not drunk with wine which leads to debauchery but be filled with the spirit"** *~Ephesians 5:18~* Just because a person has a drug or alcohol addiction doesn't mean they are bad people and it doesn't mean that they can't change. If you have a loved one with one of these addictions what they need more than anything is your support, love, and encouragement no matter what. They beat themselves up enough so they don't need anyone else to do it for them.

I also learned that arguing with them is crazy because why argue with someone, who isn't in their right mind? Engaging with them when they are under the influence may escalate the situation. Another behavior I find troubling is when individuals who are meant to support addicts record them and share information about their loved ones via text messages. Certain individuals may not see the humor in it, as their actions could potentially cause embarrassment and harm to someone they care about. Please don't be an enabler. If you know that your friend or loved one has an addiction, don't encourage them to drink with you or do drugs just because you want to have a good time from their entertainment. That's not cool and that says a lot about your character that you would use a loved one for laughs. Don't forget you may reap what you sow one day because who to say you won't switch places with that person one day or maybe you may have a child that ends up the same way so be kind always and stop making fun of addicts. *"Let us behave decently, as in the daytime, not in carousing and drunkenness, not in sexual immorality and debauchery, not in dissension and jealousy. Rather, clothe yourselves with the Lord Jesus Christ, and do not think about how to gratify the desires of the flesh." ~Romans 13:13-14~*

Chapter 12

FRIENDS IN SHEEP'S CLOTHING

A lot of women like me grew up wanting to have a lot of friends and trusting people that we called friends. I learned that a lot of us call too many people friends and not everyone is meant to be called a friend but an associate. I'm going to talk about some of my experiences with some females who I thought were my friends only to find out that they weren't. **"Even my close friend, someone I trusted, one who shared my bread, has turned against me" ~ Psalm 41:9~** I had to learn the hard way growing up because I always had a bunch of people around me who I thought genuinely cared for me but that wasn't always the case. I remember when I got my first car, I was riding my family and friends around and taking them places and we were just having a good time. I wrecked my car in my 11th grade year of high school which was also the same year that I received my car from my sister. I noticed that as soon as I wrecked my car the ones that I was hanging out with daily and riding around no longer were answering the phone or calling me. Some of them even decided to share things that I shared with them with people who were considered my enemy. That hurt me so bad because I realized even if they are family or a friend, they don't always care about you and only care about what you can do for them. *"Do not rely on a friend, do not trust in a companion. Seal the doors of your mouth from her who lie in your arms" ~Micah 7:5~* I'm the type of person who will give you the clothes off my back if you need them, but I realized that everyone isn't like me. When I went to college, I was excited because one of my best friends was also going to the same college and I knew that we would have a good time together. This situation involved choosing between two friends due to an ultimatum given by one of them after feeling betrayed by the other. I chose to remain friends with the one I had known the longest, we went to the same church, and I even dated her brother at one time. I felt like I made the right choice until we left our hometown and started college together in Montgomery, Alabama. Once the semester started, I had everything I needed but my hometown friend whom I will call Erin. Erin didn't have her books because she hadn't received her school loan yet. It was crucial for Erin to have her books as the semester had already started. She asked me if I could purchase her books for her and she would pay me back once she got her loan, so of course being the friend that I am I loaned her the money. Shortly after I lent her the money, she befriended Nita who is from the same county as our hometown, leading to a change in behavior towards me. In passing Nita mentioned that Erin had no intention of paying me back. I received a call from Erin a few days later telling me that I could come to pick up the money she borrowed from me. My spirit told me something wasn't right, and I could tell Erin was up to something because she kept asking if I was coming by myself. That's when I made the decision to bring my sister and her best friend with me to pick up the money from Erin. To make the story short Erin not only didn't give me the money back that she borrowed from me and "stated that she didn't have the money" when I arrived at her apartment complex. Erin tried to set me up that day to get jumped by her, Nita, and another girl from our hometown that I would call Sasha. Things didn't go as planned and just let's say she didn't win the battle and her friends weren't able to help her as she thought. I never got my money back, but I learned a lesson that day, you can't trust everyone, and everyone is not your friend. *" Let everyone guard against his neighbor; do not trust any brother, for every brother deals craftily, and every friend spreads slander" ~ Jeremiah 9:4~*

A few years later I started

working at Olive Garden as a server. I was surrounded by several college students and other females my age so of course I got invited to go out with some of them at times. I started hanging out with this girl I will call Whitney every weekend. We started hanging out just about daily. We would go shopping together, house parties and even the club together. Whitney stayed with her mother at the time, and they were having some problems with each other, so Whitney's mother kicked her out of the house. Being the person I am, I volunteered to let her move in with me and I even let her use my extra Verizon phone since she no longer had a phone since her mom was paying her phone bill. I noticed once Whitney started staying with me, the guy I was dealing with at the time whom I will call Seth would only come over to my house when she wasn't there, or he would just come to pick me up while she was there, and I would go to his house to spend time with him. Then my sister told me that she didn't trust Whitney because she was always walking around half-naked in front of my roommate's boyfriend, and she felt like that was disrespectful even though my roommate never said it was a problem. I listened to my sister and talked to Whitney about wearing appropriate clothing when the company was at our apartment. I was enjoying Whitney staying with me because she understood me, and I understood her. One night we decided to go out to the club, but when we arrived the line was so long and it was freezing and both of us were dressed half naked so I made the decision to leave and go home, but Whitney wanted to stay and said she would ride back with a friend. I noticed a guy that I was previously dating and intimate with in the past in line at the club as well but on the opposite side of us, so I told Whitney who he was so that she wouldn't end up talking to him because that's just the friend code. You don't mess with each other's exes or whoever your friend is dating at the time.

After I pointed Quan out to Whitney I left and went home. A few days later Whitney's old phone rang the one that I lent her before she finally bought another one, but she wasn't home. I answered the phone, and I heard Quan's voice say, "Hey Whit What's up with you" and I spazzed out. He started apologizing saying he had no idea she was my friend and I believed him, but I did know that Whitney knew who he was because I pointed him out to her so that made me feel like she purposely approached him when I left the club. When Whitney came home, I confronted her, we had a physical altercation and I kicked her out of my apartment. That was the end of that friendship. Seth told me later that Whitney also tried to come on to him and that's why he wouldn't come around when she was there. He didn't tell me because he knew that would hurt me. A lot of times other people like my sister will notice things that we are blinded to so make sure you observe who you let in your circle. I have been betrayed my whole life by people who call themselves my friend or even family members and that is the reason I learned to stop being so trustworthy and calling everyone my friend because the truth is a lot of people are secretly jealous of you. Pay attention to the so-called friends who never congratulate you on accomplishments, who sneak diss but say they are playing, and be careful who you bring around your man because a Jezebel is always lurking and calling you a friend. Booker T. Washington said something that stood out to me: " *Associate yourself with people of good quality, for it is better to be alone than in bad company.* "Now that I'm older I'm not surprised that I was hurt by people who I thought cared about me and called my friend because the same thing happened to Jesus. He was pouring into his disciples daily and Judas still betrayed him. At one point in Jesus's life, he thought of Judas as a friend, but Judas didn't feel the same way about Jesus, or it wouldn't have been so easy to betray Jesus for thirty pieces of silver. Jesus could have killed Judas if he wanted to because he knew the betrayal was coming but instead, he let God deal with Judas because he knew that the war was not with flesh and blood but against Satan himself. Jesus replied, *"The one who has dipped his hand into the bowl with me will betray me"* ~ *Matthew 26:23~* So many friends in sheep's clothing don't even realize the enemy is only setting them up to do his dirty work, but they will reap what they sow. I have no regrets about being their friend because my heart and intentions were pure. I have no idea if they ever regretted what they did to me because none of them have ever apologized but I no longer want it or need it anyway. It just was a lesson that I had to learn that some friends are dressed in sheep's clothing. *"Walk with the wise and become wise, for a companion of fools suffers harm."* ~ *Proverbs 13:20~*

Chapter 13

WOMEN DESERVE NOT TO BE VIOLATED

I have been violated too many times by younger and older men in my past and present and I don't understand why people think they can say and do things to you that are not okay. I'm writing this to stand up for all women and let them know that they are loved, cherished, and believed and never to be afraid to tell their stories. This post will be about how I was violated in my past and present, so women know that we must always be guarded no matter who the person is. We must be careful not to be by ourselves with certain individuals if we can help it. If you see or hear something that makes you feel uncomfortable take that as a warning to follow your instinct. Even though this post is for women, the same thing goes for men because a woman can also violate a man. If you have never watched the movie "Antwone Fisher" that came out in 2002 check it out and you will see exactly what I'm talking about. *"I am not what happened to me. I am what I choose to become."* ~ **Carl Jung**~ I remember the first time I felt disrespected and violated was when I was dating this guy, I would call Derrick and he invited me and one of my female cousins to hang out with him and one of his guy friends. He gave us the address so once we got there, we noticed that it was a house full of people who were family members of Derrick. Derrick walked me down the hall to a room where me and him would be hanging out and my cousin was hanging out with his male friend who I did know. Derrick walked out of the room to use the bathroom and when he did, one of his male cousins whom I will call Jeremiah entered the room and asked if I would sleep with him. I don't remember everything that I said but I do know I cursed him out and let him know that I wasn't a slut or easy girl, and he responded by walking out of the room. The crazy thing is when I look back at it I never told Derrick what happened but deep down I feel like he already knew anyway. I feel like they were testing me to see if I would sleep with both at the same time or If I was a slut and would cheat on him, but either way, I didn't like that feeling and I was shocked that it even happened. That made me look at Derrick differently too and I knew I no longer could date him. ***"When someone isn't treating you right, no matter how much you love them, you've got to love yourself more and walk away"~HealthyPlace.com~*** The second time I was violated was by a male who I looked at as my second father whom I will call Ronny because he helped my mom raise my sister and me since I was a little girl, so I completely trusted him. I remember it like it was yesterday, we were playing around the house like we always have. My mom was at work so we knew we could do things that she normally wouldn't allow such as running through the house and having a water balloon fight. So, that's exactly what we were doing. I remember splashing Ronny so well with the water balloon and I took off running afterward. He chased me around the house until he caught me and when he did, he grabbed his water balloon and he put it down my pants but when he did it he caressed my vagina at the same time. After that, I stopped playing with him because it made me feel uncomfortable even though he pretended like he didn't mean to do it. A few nights after that I remember it being hot in the house and he came into my room when I was half asleep and asked me if I was hot. I said yes thinking he would turn on the air conditioner but instead, he started licking my breasts and I told him to stop and he did. My mom was in the room sleeping and had no idea it happened and a few days later I remember my mom kicking him out of the house because she found out that he was back using crack. I didn't tell my mom that happened to me until I was in my 30s and living in North Carolina where I reside now.

She was hurt and confused and didn't understand why I didn't tell her but honestly, it was so many different reasons. I felt like if I told on him one of my parents or sister might kill him and I didn't want to lose them to the system. I also knew that Ronny was not in his right mind since he was using drugs again and I know some people may not understand this but I have no hatred towards him because he was always good to me and showed me things my father didn't show me at times. I also even questioned if anyone would even believe me because I know family members who have been molested and raped but it was always kept a secret and that is why I'm speaking out for myself and others because it is not okay. Ronny is no longer living and he died a painful death by being burnt up in a house during a fire so he reaped what he sowed at the end of the day. *"Don't be ashamed of your story… it will inspire others"* A few years later. My mom started dating this man I will call Melvin. I remember her asking me and one of my female cousins who was living with us at the time what we thought about him. We liked him because he didn't smoke or drink alcohol and he even went to church faithfully and he could quote bible verses like it was nothing. I thought he would be good for my mom even though she was still grieving from her mom and Ronny's death. I noticed things started changing once he moved into our household. He didn't want my boyfriend at the time to come to our house and he would purposely unplug the phone so I couldn't communicate with him so he thought, but my dad had bought me a cell phone so I still had a prepaid phone he didn't know about. Melvin talked my mom out of leaving all of our family behind in Alabama and moving to Florida with him where he was from. Once we moved there he started showing his true colors. I would wake up to Melvin in the bed with me, and that startled me so badly. I remember screaming and then I jumped over him and ran into the bathroom and locked the door for a while. Melvin would even kiss me on my lips and I would tell my mom and she would talk to him and he would say I just remind him of his younger daughter so much that he forgets that I'm in 11th grade. He violated me multiple times but he never molested or raped me but it got to the point my sister had to come pick me up from Florida because I no longer could live in that house. I never understood why a grown man would even be looking at me that way because I have always been small and back then I wore a size 0 to 1 so ladies please be careful who you let around your kids rather you have a daughter or son. *"Our lives begin to end the day we* **become silent about things that matter"** ~ **MartinLuther King, JR.** I have put those things that happened to me in my past behind me and I'm moving forward and using my testimonies to help others. This happened when I was 40 years old and happily married, yet older men still gaze at me as if I'm just a piece of meat.

Recently, I have been told by a man who is old enough to be my grandad that I was beautiful and that I would never want for anything as long as he was around. This man knows that I'm married and is supposed to be a close friend of our family. He even mentioned how younger girls my age like sugar daddies and I told him I have never been one of those women interested in dating an older guy who is old enough to be my father. I was riding with him in the car to a school event because I trusted him and he bluntly asked me if I knew what he would do to me if he had met me when I was younger. I responded by saying "What" and He bluntly said to me" I would have raped you" I responded by saying "And you would be in prison" and he said to me " No, I wouldn't because I would have made love to you and you would have fallen in love with me." I was very shocked that he said that to me and it triggered some of the old things that I posted above. I didn't say anything after that because I was riding in the car with him at this point but trust me he will never disrespect me like that again and I refuse to let anyone else no matter how old they are. I didn't make good judgment and I never should have ridden in the car with him since I'm a married woman even though he was supposed to be a friend of the family. When he first made some of the comments about my appearance I should have immediately put him in his place but because of his age I held back so I'm telling your ladies no matter who it is or the age speak up for yourself. Don't give them your power by allowing them to silence your voice. Your testimony just like mine will help someone else. Ladies, I don't care where you go or who you are with protect yourself at all costs. Get you a gun and keep your guard up at all times. I'm tired of people making excuses for these pedophiles so we have to stand up for each other, our rights, and for ourselves because who else is going to fight for us better than ourselves? "We do learn so much about ourselves in our experiences. *But also, know that it shouldn't have happened. This was not a lesson you needed to learn." ~Jordan Pickell~*

Chapter 14

DON'T BEAT YOURSELF UP

I decided to write this post because so many people like me are constantly beating themselves up for mistakes that we make. Sometimes we get upset with ourselves when we feel like we should have made a better decision after something didn't go as planned or it could be we beat ourselves up because we lose self-control and let someone get us out of character. We are all human and none of us are perfect, so we must learn to let things go and move on even when we feel defeated. I am one of those people who constantly beat myself up when I feel like I let the enemy win, and this is something that I'm still growing from, but it has gotten easier for me since I'm learning not to dwell on it. One of the first things I always say we should do in the morning is *Ephesians 6:10* *"Finally, be strong in the Lord and the strength of his power. Put on the whole armor of God, so that you may be able to stand against the wiles of the devil.*" but this is easier said than done. I try to read my Bible, pray, and complete at least one devotion every morning but sometimes that doesn't always happen. I also know that's something that all of you may not be able to do daily because life happens. We never know what the next day will bring. For example, you may wake up late so now you're late for work or your kids are late for school so now everyone is rushing in the morning, and reading your Bible or praying hasn't even crossed your mind. These are the times when it's easy to get irritated because you started your day off without God and Jesus. If you think about it and you're rushing trying to at least say a small prayer even if it's to yourself. I know some people feel like they aren't good at praying and not sure how to even put on the arm of God and that's okay we all must start somewhere. Here is a small prayer you can pray in the morning that I got from the **Billy Graham Training Center at the Cove website** *"Father, help us to prepare for any battle we may face. Help us to keep our eyes focused on Jesus. As we go through today, help us to stand strong and not live in fear of the enemy. Please, Lord, equip me today with the armor of God."* There comes a time in our lives when we must make decisions regarding different things; sometimes we will make good choices and other times we may not. God will always give you the answer, but we don't always listen to that voice and instead, we let our flesh take control and then later we have regrets. I heard God tell me one day when I get my taxes to put it up and not spend it and I remember telling my husband that but once I got my taxes which wasn't much, I forgot all about what God told me and instead I paid any debts that I had because I don't like being late or owing anyone for anything. Later, I came to regret that decision and I beat myself up because I found out right after that my car was considered a total loss and all I could think about was I should have waited before I spent my taxes, and I would have a car right now. I still don't have a car and it bothers me because I don't like depending on anyone for anything and if it was up to me, I never would have. This is the time when I must trust God because it's not easy and I cry all the time. I felt like I let God down because I knew what he told me, and I forgot all about it as soon as the money came. I don't like it when I'm disobedient to God. I'm telling you just like I constantly tell myself there is no point in beating yourself up and dwelling on it because the decision has been made and nothing can be done about it now. No matter how much we beat ourselves up it's not going to change the situation. ***"Don't carry your mistakes around with you*. Instead, place them under your feet and use them as** *stepping stones" ~ Unknown~* Every one of us knows a person that is difficult to get along with and those are the type of people that we normally try to stay from around. There are certain people that you just can't avoid, and you must be around them because you are in the same circle, meaning you may work at the same company, live near each other, or it's a blended family member, etc. We must learn how to handle being around those types of individuals because if not we may end up doing something that we may regret later. I have been in that situation so many times with an individual that I don't like because I feel like she is Satan's daughter, and no one can tell me different. So many times, I have had encounters with this person, and I would ignore her and laugh at her when she would say things to try to get under my skin, but everyone knows that when it comes to my son, husband, parents, or sister I will read you to filth and the devil knows that as well. This same person has even played on my phone at 3 am like we're in high school and I still ignored her childish behavior. She crossed the line when she started talking recklessly to my husband and then she brought my son into the conversation as well and that's what made me tick. I remember calling her and telling her to talk to me the way she was talking to my husband but of course she wouldn't and instead, she kept hanging up the phone before she did, she threatened to put her hands on me. I don't take kindly to threats so when she saw me the next time, I made sure I spoke to her on purpose. I wanted to see if she was going to put action with her words but of course, all she did was run her mouth and she got right back in her car before I got active. I'm not going to lie and act like it didn't make me feel good because it did. After all, for some people, you must let them know they don't scare you, which I did exactly that. I later felt bad about it only because I was like why did I let someone like her get me out of character? She is a non-factor in my eyes, and she always will be. I still have to see this individual at times, and I always will unless

God has a different plan for my life but I vowed to myself not to fall for the devil's scheme again and also not to beat myself up if I do get out of character now and then because some people truly deserve it but I know God can handle them way better than we can. Stop beating yourself up! We are all a work and progress, which means we get there a little at a time, not all at once. Here's a quote for all of us to remember **by Royalebradin** *"Stop beating yourself up for what you didn't do right in the past, without those mistakes you wouldn't know how to move forward now"*

Chapter 15

BOUNDARIES ARE NECESSARY

What does it mean to set personal boundaries? According to the University of California, Berkeley website *Personal boundaries are the limits and rules we set for ourselves within relationships.* I have found out that setting boundaries is necessary for your mental health. I didn't realize that so many of my problems came because I wasn't setting boundaries with people. My therapist recommended that I read a book called **"Set Boundaries, Find Peace: A Guide to Reclaiming Yourself" By Nedra Glover Tawwab,** that book changed my life forever. I shared the book with some of my friends, and family, and even on social media because I wanted to help others the way that book helped me. One of my cousins even formed a book club after reading that book. I'm so glad that my therapist recommended that book to me because if she wouldn't there is no telling how long I would have continued to let things slide when I needed to speak up for myself. Nedra Glover Tawwab stated that her definition of boundaries are expectations and needs that help you feel safe and comfortable in your relationships. Expectations in relationships help you stay mentally and emotionally well. Learning when to say no and when to say yes is also an essential part of feeling comfortable when interacting with others. One boundary that I had to set was what I would tolerate from others and what I wouldn't tolerate due to my mental health. I had to set a boundary with a loved one that I would no longer allow them to call me when they were under the influence of alcohol because I didn't like hearing them sound sluggish and sometimes when they were under the influence if I disagreed with whatever they were saying they would get upset with me and start talking to me aggressively. At times, we would get into an argument, or

I would hang up the phone and then I would get crazy text messages afterward. So, one day when they were sober, I had a conversation with the person, and I said that when you're drinking, please do not call or text me. If you do, I will hang up the phone as soon as I hear the slur in your voice and if you text me something crazy because you are under the influence I'm not even going to read the text I'm going to immediately delete it. I said we can't ride to functions together if you're going to be drinking. It was a hard decision to make but I knew that I couldn't keep tolerating it. ***"Make every effort to live in peace with everyone and to be holy; without holiness, no one will see the Lord." ~Hebrews 12:14 NIV~*** Sometimes you must learn to set boundaries when people are constantly asking you to borrow money. This is a boundary that I had to learn to set with others. I had friends and family calling me all the time asking me if they could borrow money from me, and I would always give it to them. There were times when I didn't have it, but I would still give it to them because I hated not to give it knowing they needed it. Doing that only made me an enabler and some of them kept mishandling their finances recklessly because they knew they could always call me if needed. My last straw was when I told a family member that my husband and I were going on vacation for our Anniversary and within a few minutes of telling her that, she asked me to borrow money. I thought that was very disrespectful and selfish, especially knowing that I just said we were going on vacation. I wasn't sure exactly how much money I would spend on my trip because I knew I would be buying souvenirs and going to different shopping places and restaurants. At that moment it was like a light bulb went off in my head and I told her "No, I don't have it to give" After that, I started learning to say no more often. That isn't telling a lie because it just means I may have the money, but I don't have the money to give out to someone else. I don't mind helping others and I still help some people from time to time, but I had to learn that some people will take advantage of your kindness for weakness. Sometimes people will even borrow money from you with no intention of paying you back at times, so make sure you set boundaries with people like that. *"Stop asking* **why they keep doing it and start asking why you keep allowing it" ~ Unknown~ "Givers need to set limits** *because takers rarely do"* **~Rachel Wolchin~** Another boundary I had to set with some of my family members was to mind their business. All families have disagreements and that's normal but if they put God. First, they will always find their way back to each other is what I believe. A few family members and I have disagreed at different times in my life, and I have decided not to talk to them for a certain amount of time due to my feelings being hurt by some of the things they said to me. Due to a lack of communication and misunderstanding. I'm not always good at expressing my feelings with words and I felt like some of them weren't even trying to hear me out, so I said I was done trying with a few family members due to that reason and some of them have hurt my feelings more than once. I decided to distance myself and love them from a distance until I was ready to have a conversation with them again. I constantly prayed for them and God to repair our relationship. I had family members calling me telling me that I and the family member I was upset with needed to make amends with each other and how I needed to be the bigger person since. I was supposed to be a Christian. Some of them even tried to use bible scriptures to manipulate me to talk to the person. And then I had one family member even say I needed to forgive the other person due to them being more sensitive than me like that made a difference. Every time I have chosen to distance myself from any of my family members one of my other family members will always call me saying different things to try to get me to speak to the person and it started irritating me. I felt like they weren't respecting my feelings or my boundaries. I didn't care to explain myself to them because it was none of their business it was between me and the other person. I finally told them certain words weren't said to you that were said to me by that person, so you will never understand. I also had to tell some of them that I understood that they loved both of us and I also loved that person as well but right now I am hurt, and my feelings are valid and you or no one else will tell me otherwise. I told them I was asking them nicely to respect my boundaries and that right now I didn't feel like speaking or seeing the other person. Whenever I am ready I would. In our timing and not anyone else. So, they understood how serious I was about my boundaries. I also said to them "When you have had disagreements with people and chose not to speak to them for a certain period, I never got in the middle of it" I am asking you to do the same. I said if you can't stay out of the middle of it then I have no choice but to distance myself from you as well until you can learn to respect my boundaries and my feelings. I hated to do that but sometimes you just must set those types of boundaries and when I set that boundary after that with all of them no one ever got in my business again. *"Setting boundaries is not about keeping people away,* **rather it is a powerful act of self-care." ~ Michelle Maros~**

Chapter 16

PREGNANCY LOSS

Many women are suffering in silence due to losing a child or children. A lot of people don't realize that there are so many ways that a woman can lose a child. Just to name a few, some different pregnancy losses include complete miscarriage, inevitable miscarriage, stillbirth, septic, blighted ovum, and ectopic pregnancy loss, etc. I decided to write on this topic because I suffered from an ectopic pregnancy. Until this happened to me, I didn't even know what an ectopic pregnancy was, and I didn't realize that so many women have lost children in other ways besides miscarriage or stillbirth which were the only two I was aware of. *An ectopic pregnancy is when a fertilized egg implants itself outside of the womb, usually in one of the fallopian tubes. The fallopian tubes are the tubes connecting the ovaries to the womb. If an egg gets stuck in them, it won't develop into a baby and your health may be at risk if the pregnancy continues.* Below, I'm going to tell you my story about how I lost my babies. Losing a child is one of the most painful experiences a person can endure. In September 2017, I started feeling sick and it lasted for days so I finally decided to go to the emergency room. Once I got there and they ran different tests the nurse came in the room and told me that I was pregnant with twins. I almost fell out of the chair. I was shocked. I knew twins ran in my family, but I wasn't expecting to be the one pregnant with twins and I wasn't even trying to get pregnant. I had just started back on birth control only to find this out. To be honest, when I first found out I wasn't that excited about it because my husband already had 3 kids and I had 1 so to me 4 was the perfect number of kids. We already had two boys and two girls together. Growing up I always said I wanted 4 boys, but I was happy with the 4 kids I already had. When I told my husband that I was pregnant. His response was "I already knew" and he didn't seem upset about it so that helped me. I figured this was God's plan. Even though we weren't trying to get pregnant, I was excited about my babies. I made an appointment to have an ultrasound done and my husband was supposed to go with me but got called in to work. My mother-in-law said she would go with me, and she told my husband not to call out of work, so he didn't. When I got ready to go to my appointment my mother-in-law told me that she wasn't going to make it after all and now my feelings are hurt but I said there will be other ones. I got to the doctor's office and was waiting for my results for the ultrasound but instead, several nurses and doctors kept coming in and out of my room. After 30 minutes went by, I could tell something was wrong by their facial expressions. After about an hour of waiting I was told that I had an ectopic pregnancy and that they had to take my babies because it could be life-threatening to me. Hearing that news hurt me so bad and then having to hear it alone made it even worse. *"The Lord gave, and the Lord has taken away; bless be the name of the Lord." ~ Job 1:21~* As soon as I left the hospital, I sat in my car, and I cried and then I called my husband and cried even more. My husband was so supportive, and I believe that's what helped me get through this, to be honest. "He told me that if losing the babies meant saving my life that's what was most important to him because I wasn't replaceable" The hospital referred me to another place to go to so that they could start treating me for the ectopic pregnancy. I was given the medication methotrexate to take. This medication stops cell growth and dissolves existing cells. The medication was given to me by injection, and I had to stay at the hospital for hours and then I was released. Even though I was given that medication I didn't lose my babies immediately. For months, I had to go to the doctor's office weekly and give blood work so they could see if I had lost the babies and every time they were still there and then finally one month later one of the babies was gone. It broke my heart having to go weekly seeing other women pregnant when I knew I no longer could have my babies. I finally lost the other baby months later but I'm not sure exactly when it happened. I just know that whenever I went for blood work the baby had passed. I was bleeding so much I couldn't tell if it was the baby coming out or just heavy bleeding. *"So do not fear, for I am with you; do not be dismayed, for I am your God. I will strengthen you and help you; I will uphold you with my righteous right hand""* ~ *Isaiah 41:10~* During my grieving time, I was so angry at God, and I remember telling him that I hated him, and I just couldn't understand why he would give me babies that I didn't ask for only to take them from me. I remember crying daily from the time I woke up until I went back to sleep. My husband was there for me as much as he could but that didn't matter to me because I wanted my babies that I had just lost. I felt robbed. I remember one morning at about 3 am I was lying on the floor crying as my husband and son slept. I remember hearing God tell me to read the chapter Job. I got up and went into the living room. I opened my Bible and turned to the Job chapter, and I remember not stopping until I read the entire chapter. After I read it, I felt like some weight was lifted off my shoulders and I remember apologizing to God for all the things I said mean to him even though I knew God knew it was coming from a broken heart. I still cry but just not daily but when September comes since that's the month I lost my babies, when May comes because that's when my due date was as well as it's the month Mother's Day is in. I no longer blame God and I know that he doesn't make any mistakes. I try to think about it positively now. For example, I tell myself maybe God knew that my babies would have some type of medical condition and that would bring more stress on me, etc. When you go through the disappointment of losing a child sometimes you feel alone and don't feel like anyone understands your pain. When you are feeling like that, I advise you to call and talk to a friend or family member, or join a social media Pregnancy loss group or group in your area that has other women who have lost a child so that you have someone who can relate to your pain. You can also send a text to the number **719-626-8486** and connect with somebody who's been in your shoes or you can go to their website ***https://www.foreknownministries.org/women#WEIGH and they have an eBook you can even download called "Where do I go from here"*** If you have experienced pregnancy loss give yourself time to grieve and grieve in your own time and your own way no matter what anyone else says. ***"The Lord is close to the brokenhearted; He* rescues those whose spirits are crushed"**. **~Psalm 34:18~**

Chapter 17

BEING PATIENT WITH GOD

We need to learn to stop being in a hurry all the time and wanting things to happen immediately. God is an on-time God, not an our-time God so we have to learn to be patient. I feel like I have expected things to happen on my time for the majority of my entire life even when things weren't going well. I still expected God to fix things immediately but that's not how things work. When we rush God that's when things go wrong and when we try to take matters into our hands and go before God that's when we cause ourselves to have a major setback. The enemy knows that we want things to happen immediately and that's why he starts putting all kinds of crazy thoughts in our heads and making us feel like we have to take control of things instead of waiting on God. Satan knows that we are so close to our blessing and that's why he purposely gets in our mind. When this happens we have to learn to tune him out. When we feel like we are getting impatient with God, that's when we have to pray even harder and continue to focus one day at a time and not think about things that haven't come up yet. *"Listen to counsel and receive instruction. That you may be wise in your latter days. There are many plans in a man's heart nevertheless the Lord's counsel that will stand" ~ Proverbs 19:20-21~* I don't believe that there is anyone on this earth who hasn't tried to do things without waiting for God to give them instructions. We have been programmed to feel like we have to be in control of everything or it won't work out. So many people have fallen in love with someone or were infatuated with someone that God told them to stay away from maybe because they were married, a drug dealer, abusive, or just broken but they didn't listen because they just felt like the person God was telling them to stay away from were too good to be true only to find out the reason God told them to stay away from them only to be shattered and broken years later. After all, you chose to not listen to counsel when you know in your heart that God told you to stay away from that person. I have also been one of those people knowing God told me that a guy was unequally yoked for me but I still chose to be in a relationship with him, because I felt like they were so attractive and looked good on my arm and because they were able to cater to things that I wanted so I didn't have to spend my own money even though I could if needed. Only to regret dating them years later but if I had been patient with God until he brought a healthy healed person into my life I wouldn't have gone through that heartbreak and could have been one step closer to meeting my husband or just enjoying my life during that time instead of laying in my bed crying at night about a person God told me not to date in the first place. Or it could be that you're in a relationship with a good hard-working person but they are going through a hard time at the moment and they aren't able to buy you the wedding ring you deserve so they want to wait to propose while they are saving up their money, and you know God has told you this person is for you but instead, you feel like he/she isn't getting his/her finances and other things in order fast enough so you decide to leave him/her for another person only to find out they can't keep a job and constantly lies about everything and now you have lost the person that God told you to be patient with all because you lost patient and didn't want to listen to the spirit and instead let your flesh lead "***Sometimes God doesn't meet our expectations because he wants to exceed them. "~ Sharon Jaynes~*** There are a lot of people at jobs that are in positions lower than where they deserve to be. I have been in that position before as well. Where you feel like you're constantly going on interviews at the company you work for so you can be promoted to a higher level but the position keeps going to someone else.Of course, it would break my heart every single time I was told I didn't get the position, especially when I knew I was better than the person that got the position over me. I had to learn that God may just have a better position for me that is even better than that one. I've known people who have worked at a job for years only to feel unappreciated because they felt like the company they worked for didn't appreciate the hard work and overtime they were doing so they put in their resignation only to find out they were just about to be offered the position. We have to learn to be patient and not expect things to happen immediately. There are so many people in the bible who had to wait 40-plus years to receive some of their blessings. They may have had to wait a long time and go through some trials and tribulations but when the blessing came it was better than they could even imagine. *"Rejoice in hope, be patient in tribulation, be constant in prayer." ~ Romans 12:12~* Even when it comes to making decisions for your family. Many times, I said I wanted to leave North Carolina and move closer to Alabama or Georgia since that's where most of my family lives. It's not about me though; I can't just up and move because of my selfish reasons when I know God hasn't told me to leave yet. It also affects my entire family. If we were to move then that would mean my son would have to leave all his friends that he started with since Kindergarten just because I wanted to be closer to family, not because a job offered me or my husband to move due to God blessing one of us with a new job or because God told us it's time to make a change. If I hadn't been patient we could have made the mistake of moving away and ended up in a bad neighborhood that we thought was a good neighborhood by pictures we saw online or we could have moved into a place and ended up not even liking it or not liking our neighbors. Etc. Make sure that God is in every decision that you make. We have to be patient and not be quick to make decisions out of fear, selfishness, spitefulness, or impatience. *"Those who leave everything in God's hand will eventually see God's hand in everything."* ~ *Unknown~*

Chapter 18

MEN ARE NOT ALWAYS THE PROBLEM

Over these last few years, I have realized that men are not always the problem. I used to always believe that men were the abusers, liars, deadbeats, and so much more due to things that I have experienced in my life and witnessed female family members go through with a man, but as I have matured and observed I have realized that some of us women are also abusers, liars, deadbeats, manipulators, and so much more. We always want to point the figure at the man instead of owning our mess and that's why God put it in my spirit to write this blog post because I don't support women who are like that. I am a girl's girl and will support my women as much as I can, but right is right and wrong is wrong and it's time that someone stands up for our men. So many women use their children as pawns against their children's fathers, and to me that is the devil's work so if you are one of those women you need to get saved, go to therapy, and grow up. I talk to so many women who would say their kid's fathers are deadbeats and don't do anything for their kids only to find out that the father wasn't a deadbeat, and that the woman was just mad because he chose to live a life that didn't include her.According to Google, *a deadbeat is a person who deliberately avoids paying debts or neglects responsibilities* so if you are calling your child or children's father a deadbeat and he is paying child support, calling his child or children over the phone or texting them constantly, going to school events, and spending time with them they are not a deadbeat. There is only so much that a person can do and take from a person who is just wicked and bitter. I have witnessed my husband and other male family members face ongoing obstacles when attempting to spend quality time with their kids. Although they faithfully provide financial support and try to communicate in-person and by phone with their children. I've heard countless stories of men going to the courthouse and requesting to be put on child support due to the custodial parent calling them a deadbeat when they are upholding the financial agreement they agreed upon without the courts. What I've realized is that women who hurt their children's fathers on purpose are either resentful that their ex-partner has moved on physically and emotionally or they are grieving the loss of a good man. Some examples of the toxic behavior I've witnessed firsthand. First, the custodial parent/mother would often send the non-custodial parent/father pictures of the children early in the morning or late at night during the work week.There is nothing wrong with sending pictures of your kids when they are school-aged or younger but at 6 am in the morning or midnight is inconsiderate and comes across as intentional. Especially when it's regularly.

" So many parents are blind to the fact that when they're trying to hurt their ex, they're really only hurting their child. What a beautiful world it would be if parents truly put their child's well-being ahead of their revenge agenda" ~ *Jenna Korf~*

Another example is a close friend of mine witnessed. The father reached out to the mother to coordinate the date, time, and location for his court-ordered routine visits. Mother shows up at the pickup location mid-day dressed in nightclub attire, makes flirtatious comments and appears to make an advance at the father. The father declines her advances, and she becomes verbally agitated in front of the children. Another incident, surrounding court-ordered visitations involved the mother refusing to allow the kids to leave with their father when she noticed his wife and stepchild were in his car. These types of women don't care that they are hurting their children. Now, the father must witness his kids crying because they no longer can go with him. Then women will call their friends and family members and tell lies about the child's father to destroy his character all because he didn't beg you like you wanted him to or didn't acknowledge what you had on. I encourage involved fathers to seek joint custody, even if you are on good terms today, because that may change once you have moved on. Women, there comes a point in our life where we have to grow up and realize that just because we have a child by a man doesn't mean he's going to stay and doesn't mean that he is a bad person just because he no longer wants to be in a relationship with you. We also need to stop blaming our kid's father's new partner for his decision-making when he stands up to you. A man is not a doormat, and he has a mind of his own and can make his own decisions. Whether some of you women realize it or not, Parent Alienation is Emotional Abuse.

"You can hide behind your lies all day, but one day you will have to explain to your child why you hated the other parent more than you loved them"~ssac2010.wordpress.com~ Women we can't control who our ex has around our kids. The way you have the right to bring whomever you want around your kids he also has the right to do the same. A father should never have to go to court for visitation to see his kids because she is mad that he has a certain person around them even though that person has never done anything to you or your kids. We women will bad mouth our kids' fathers to our kids just to make them see their father in a bad light not knowing that karma is real and what goes around comes around. To the men reading this continue to be the wonderful father that you are, let God deal with this unhealed person because only he can save their deceitful soul. The kids may believe their mother at the moment

because that's who they live with but once they get older they will start seeing things for themselves and if they never do all you can do is pray one day they will but never stop living your life because that's what the enemy wants you to do. ***"He shouldn't have to fight this hard or even fight to see his child" ~Unknown~*** Lastly, Women we need to stop putting our hands on men and then playing the victim when they react. It's neither right for a man to physically assault a woman nor is it right for a woman to physically assault a man. Neither one of us is better than the next person. If a man walks away from you during an argument let him go. Stop chasing him and give him his space. Also, stop fighting and being toxic in front of your kids because you are showing them that this lifestyle is okay when it isn't. We women will provoke that man and then say he's not a real man, no you aren't a mature woman and need to let go of your childish ways. If you think putting your hands on a man is cute and you laugh about it with your friends it says a lot about the person that you are inside and you need to do some inner work within yourself. *" Men can be victims too, women are not the only victims of domestic violence and abuse. Men also suffer from domestic abuse, especially verbal and emotional abuse, and maybe even more ashamed to seek help" ~ Unknown~*

Chapter 19

STRUGGLES OF TEENAGERS

I decided to write this blog post because, as a teenager, I faced silent struggles. I have talked to my teenage kids about their struggles and wanted to share this post to help parents recognize when their teenagers are silently struggling. It's important to observe changes in behavior as some parents may mistake signs of struggle for typical teenage behavior. They may have a negative attitude due to school issues but might not share it with parents for fear of being misunderstood or dismissed. Common teenage struggles include peer pressure about being sexually active, their physical appearance, social status in school,consuming alcohol and illegal drugs, and academic pressure. Teenagers go through a lot of peer pressure from their friends at times about having sex and body issues. I remember when I was in high school a lot of my friends were having sex, but I hadn't lost my virginity at the time and one friend would tell me that having sex was one of the best feelings in the world and how I was missing out. I remember telling her "I'm good" and she kept telling me that I was scary. The guy I was talking to at the time wanted me to French kiss him and I wouldn't because I felt like it was gross, and I didn't want him sticking his tongue down my throat, so I dismissed his advances. Later, I found out that the friend who was calling me scary slept with him while I was dating him and then the next boyfriend I had she gave him oral sex. I felt so betrayed, and the boys only did that because I wouldn't have sex with them. So many girls and boys go through that with their peers still today. A lot of boys who are virgins will be told they are gay just because they don't want to have sex with a girl and there's nothing wrong with that. I wish I wouldn't have lost my virginity at a young age, but I was trying to fit in with the crowd. We must talk to our kids about sex and not the birds and bees crap. We must be straight-up honest with them and allow them to be open with us. I have been that way from day one with my kids so that way they confide in me about things without feeling embarrassed to talk about sex. If you suspect your kids may be having sex you need to give them condoms because we can't keep saying my kid wouldn't do that because your kid absolutely will. It's not permitting them to have sex. It's letting them know I don't want you to but if you choose to make that decision, I want you to practice safe sex. I know a female that became pregnant at the age of 13. She hid her pregnancy until it was time for the baby to be born. She didn't get that big and she wore baggy clothes, so she was able to hide it from her parents. She was too afraid to tell her parents because she thought they might kick her out of the house or make her have an abortion. If her parents had been observing her a little more, they may have realized she was having sex and could have prevented the teenage pregnancy by putting her on birth control and giving her condoms. *"When you say 'Yes' to others, make sure you are not saying "No" to yourself" ~Paulo Coelho~* Many kids are exposed to growing up too fast, engaging in alcohol and drug use, including vaping marijuana. School environments may not always be safe, with some students getting caught with drugs. Children may face peer pressure to smoke and drink in bathrooms or at sports events, even when parents drop them off, unaware of their activities. Parents should be cautious about their children's friends to prevent negative influences like drug and alcohol use. Children may struggle to say no to peer pressure and might not report bullying for fear of being labeled a snitch. Regularly communicate with your children to understand their experiences and watch for signs of dishonesty or distress. *"Whoever walks with the wise becomes wise, but the companion of fools will suffer harm"*

~Proverbs 13:20~ Teenage girls may feel pressured to fit in with popular peers, leading to compromising situations like sharing clothes or engaging in gossip and conflicts. It's crucial for parents to teach children about setting boundaries with friends, building self-esteem, and resisting manipulation. *"Teenagers face the stress of trying to fit into a society that doesn't always accept them for who they are ~Anonymous~*

According https://www.turnbridge.com/news-events/latest-articles/teen-suicide-facts/ suicide is the second leading cause of death for young people ages 10-24. Your child may be contemplating suicide, and you don't even know it due to teenage pressures. I was one of those kids who wanted to commit suicide at one point of time in my life. All because I was looking for love in all the wrong places. I was tired of getting cheated on by a guy and it made me have low self-esteem about myself.

My dad didn't live in the house with us, and he chose another woman and her child over my mother, me, and my sister in my eyes. I wasn't that close to him growing up, so I didn't talk to him about things. My mom was my best friend, but she was struggling with her demons due to how my father treated her, so I didn't want to feel like I was bothering her, and I didn't want to put anything else on her plate for her to have to deal with. A lot of times teenagers may feel alone in their homes even if they have people there daily and they have friends because of some things they may not want to discuss. Some kids want to commit suicide because they lost someone close to them that they feel like they couldn't live without, school stress due to the hard work, being bullied at school, rape, molestation, or dealing with a parent who is addicted to drugs and alcohol. To support teens dealing with academic pressure and personal issues, communicate openly with them, watch for warning signs like changes in behavior or self-harm, and discuss faith and Bible verses for emotional support. *" The Lord is near to the brokenhearted and saves the crushed in spirit. Many are the afflictions of the righteous, but the Lord delivers him out of them all" ~ Psalm 34:18-19*

Chapter 20

MOTHERS THAT DON'T KNOW THEIR PLACE

I have dated people whose mothers were overly involved in their lives. While I understand being protective, when a grown child's mother behaves possessively, it raises concerns. During my sophomore year of college, I encountered this situation when I began dating a guy named John, whom I later developed feelings for. Facing issues with my roommate, I realized I needed to either relocate or risk our relationship deteriorating. To preserve our friendship, I had to choose between moving out or extending our lease as it was coming to an end. I confided in the guy I was dating, contemplating living independently. He supported my decision and reassured me that he was there for me. He suggested sharing a place to reduce my expenses, which I eventually agreed to after careful consideration. At that time, he was residing with his mother. I had a great relationship with his mother as we attended church together every Sunday and took turns cooking. Since my family wasn't in Montgomery, I cherished being a part of his family. John planned to move out soon and get an apartment with me but wanted to wait until we found a place and signed the lease before telling his mother. When we found a place we both liked, he informed his mother. Unexpectedly, I received a call from John's mother pleading with me not to let him move in with me, without providing a reason, except that she believed it was best for him to stay with her. I explained that it was John's decision, and we were moving in together despite her feelings. Life was smooth sailing for me and John until things took a turn. After being together for more than four years, our relationship hit a rough patch as John faced challenges with employment. He would either quit his job due to conflicts with his boss, refusal to follow instructions or get fired for tardiness. Additionally, he was pursuing a late-night rap career. During our time residing together, there were three instances of domestic violence and infidelity. His mother would often call me, criticizing me and warning that her son might leave me if I didn't improve. During arguments, he would involve his mother, who would call me as late as 3 am, causing further tension. She consistently held me responsible for everything, even when her son was at fault. Despite presenting evidence, she would insist that her son did not hit me or damage my phone by throwing it against the wall. Feeling frustrated, I realized it was a futile situation because he was clearly favored as Mama's boy. Regardless of my actions, she always pointed fingers at me for his mistakes. Eventually, I decided he should go back to live with his mother since she seemed to prefer it that way. The complexities of this relationship, especially with his mother's involvement, could fill a book, but I will end here out of respect for the relationship that still exists to some extent. " If a mother disrespects her son's partner... It just proves that she doesn't respect her son" Not long ago, I had another experience that stands out in my memory. I began dating an incredible guy, whom I'll refer to as Quincey. His mother, unfortunately, seemed unhappy in her own life and projected this onto her children, which was disheartening. Initially, she portrayed herself as someone she wasn't and was very cordial to me, like John's mother. She would frequently call me at the start, but once her son moved in with me after leaving her home, her true nature surfaced. This guy had only lived with his mom due to a past toxic relationship and had not yet found his own place. When he met me, we transitioned from friends to something more. His mom, aware of his payday routine from their shared living situation, would consistently ask to borrow money, often substantial amounts. After numerous requests, he informed her that he needed to support his own family and couldn't continue providing her with money every payday. I was blamed for his response. She stopped contacting me, and when I reached out to her, she wouldn't respond to my calls. One day, I saw on Facebook that she was conversing with Quincy's ex-girlfriend, referring to the ex as her daughter-in-law, which deeply hurt me. Naturally, I shared my feelings with my partner. His reply was that her behavior was typical of her character and would likely persist. He mentioned that she seemed unhappy and would probably remain so, but her actions wouldn't change his feelings towards me. He assured me that he wouldn't leave me for anyone, regardless of who she talked to. This made me fall even more in love with him because I realized his love was genuine. I suggested he speak to her, but he believed it would be fruitless as she was an adult who would act as she pleased, regardless of our opinions, which turned out to be true. Quincy and I had been in a relationship for a while and were very content. One day, his mother invited us to her birthday party, and we attended. To my surprise, she had also invited a girl who had previously made advances towards Quincy, and his mother was aware of this fact. Additionally, the girl had harassed me at work since she was my colleague. This incident revealed to me that his mother was untrustworthy and didn't respect boundaries. I didn't let it affect me and had a pleasant evening with my mother, who was there with us along with the rest of the family. I simply ignored the presence of the girl. I never gave his mom any reason to treat me like that, considering all the things she had done beyond what I'm mentioning now. Perhaps one day, I'll share the complete story. *"Don't let negative and toxic people rent space in your head. Raise the rent and kick them out"* *~Robert Tew~* If you find yourself in this situation or know someone who is, here's a piece of advice: when it comes to the mother of your partner, it's best to stop trying to befriend her if she has made it clear she dislikes you. People reveal their true selves, so it's crucial to believe their actions. Remember, you are worthy of their son's affection, and you haven't done anything to deserve mistreatment. If your partner stands by you, then focus on your happiness and distance yourself from his mother. Life moves forward, with or without her presence. Some mothers may overstep boundaries because their sons have allowed it or believe they can. It's important to set boundaries and teach others how to respect you. "It's okay to cut toxic relatives out of your life. That blood ain't thicker than peace of mind'

Chapter 21

SPIRITUAL GUIDANCE TIPS

These are some spiritual guidance tips that worked for me. For some of you who don't know what spiritual guidance is according to Google, *Spiritual guidance is a confidential meeting with an experienced guide who assists you in listening to God's voice in your daily life.* The first thing you must do if you want to have a closer and deeper relationship with God is you must *read your Bible daily* no matter what. I believe that despite distractions and busyness, we prioritize what truly matters. If nurturing a relationship with God is a priority for you, then you will invest the effort. Reading the Bible can be challenging due to its complexity, but with numerous versions available, you can explore various options. Take time to research and read reviews on different Bibles until you discover one that resonates with you. Alternatively, seek recommendations from friends or family members on the type of Bible they find helpful. You can even download the *"YouVersion Bible App"* and read different versions that way. To distinguish between the flesh and the spirit, it is crucial to read and understand the Word. The Word serves as a guide to recognize when you are being led by the spirit or by your own desires. Take the initiative to study the Word independently rather than relying on others, as not everyone will offer accurate guidance; the Bible, however, always will. *Memorize bible verses* so that when you are going through things you can focus back on what it says in the Bible so that you don't make decisions off on emotions which are your flesh. For example, **Jeremiah 29:11 says,** *" For I know the plans I have for you,' declares the Lord, 'plans to prosper you and not to harm you, plans to give you a hope and a future. "* Oftentimes, unexpected events like job loss, eviction, or divorce can trigger negative thoughts such as feeling unlovable or constantly facing obstacles.

These thoughts, driven by negativity, aim to keep you stagnant. By internalizing these Bible verses, you'll realize these are falsehoods, and setbacks indicate better things ahead from God. Without a spiritual connection, it's easy to fall for the devil's lies and let negativity take over. These verses serve as your spiritual compass, guiding you toward the truth. ***Pray and talk to God*** throughout your day. Throughout the day – morning, afternoon, and night – aim to maintain your connection with God through prayer. Prayer has a powerful impact beyond what you may realize. There's no one right way to pray; you can simply converse with God as you would with a loved one, expressing your true feelings because He already knows them. The devil also listens to our prayers, underscoring the importance of a strong spiritual bond with God. This connection will help you discern when the devil tries to use something you prayed for to unsettle you. In the

Bible, **John 10:27** *says "My sheep hear my voice and I know them, and follow them, and they follow me."* If you neglect to spend time in prayer and communicate with God, distinguishing His voice from the enemy's voice becomes challenging. For instance, imagine praying for a partner who respects you, and when God sends that person your way, the devil plants doubts and insecurities in your mind. This interference can lead you to doubt the individual God has brought into your life, causing you to push them away and miss out on a blessing. By listening to your inner voice, you can discern between your earthly desires and spiritual guidance. The devil may attempt to disrupt your relationship by sending past partners unexpectedly, but by staying attuned to your spiritual intuition, you can recognize the deception and reject negative thoughts about your partner, as you are familiar with their true character from spending time together.

"Whatever is... true, noble, pure, right, admirable, lovely if anything is excellent or praiseworthy think about such things" ~ **Philippians 4:8~** *Worship and Praise* God through gospel music. Engage with gospel music that brings healing to your soul. Explore various songs until you discover one that deeply connects with you. Continue to worship and express gratitude to God by acknowledging His grace and mercy. Your spirit may communicate with you during moments of praise. Sometimes, while worshiping, unexpected tears may flow, signaling that everything will be alright as God reassures you. If you find yourself waking up in the middle of the night without reason, it could be a sign that God is reaching out to you through the spirit. Say out loud *"Speak Lord, Your servant is listening"* ~ **1 Samuel 3:8~** and sit still and the first thing that comes to mind is what God is trying to tell you. Additionally, he often confirms matters to you in three distinct ways; therefore, it's crucial

to remain attentive. Confirmation could come through a person, recurring dreams, a sermon, a Bible verse, or other means. The key is that you will always receive the initial indication, signaling that it is indeed confirmation.

Chapter 22

DOMESTIC VIOLENCE IS NOT OKAY

Domestic violence is a harrowing reality for many, and it's crucial to break the cycle by raising awareness and sharing our stories. I chose to write this blog post to stand up for all domestic violence survivors and honor those who tragically did not survive. My journey through several abusive relationships has taught me a vital lesson: it's not okay, and we must tell our stories to save others from enduring what we've endured. Your testimony, whether you realize it or not, can be a lifeline for someone else. Growing up in a household where domestic violence was prevalent, I mistakenly equated violence with love. This misconception was reinforced by seeing relatives and friends endure similar abusive dynamics. At one point, this seemed normal to me, and I know I'm not alone in having such experiences. It's important to acknowledge that not everyone is ready or able to share their stories, and that's okay. However, I hope that one day, more survivors will find the strength to speak out. We must learn to prioritize our well-being and understand that love should never come with violence. Choosing to leave an abusive relationship is incredibly challenging, especially when children are involved. Abusers often manipulate their victims, saying whatever they think will keep them from leaving. But remember, staying for the sake of a child is not a valid reason to remain in a harmful environment. You can love and forgive someone, but you must prioritize your safety and mental health by leaving and never returning. By sharing our stories and supporting each other, we can create a safer future for ourselves and others, breaking the cycle of domestic violence once and for all. *"Whoever sheds human blood, by humans shall their blood be shed; for in the image of God has God made mankind" ~ Genesis 9:6~* The first time I was physically abused was when I was in 9th grade by the guy

I lost my virginity too. I have known him since I was little because his dad and my dad were good friends, so my dad brought me around him and his family when I was younger. When we first started dating, we talked about all kinds of things, even people we had crushes on before we started dating each other. I remember going to Opp, AL with my boyfriend at the time, whom I'm going to call Clarence, and two of his sisters. We were in Opp because Clarence's oldest sister's boyfriend at the time lived there, so we were all hanging out. It was a small, tight-knit community where everyone seemed to know each other, and the atmosphere was warm and inviting. One of Clarence's younger sisters, whom I'll call Toya, asked me to walk with her around the neighborhood just to get out of the house since it was a beautiful sunny day. As Toya and I were walking around the neighborhood, we happened to come across the guy I mentioned to Clarence that I had a crush on a while back. Toya knew him, so she stopped and struck up a conversation, leaving me to stand there silently as they chatted away. When we eventually turned around to head back home, I noticed Clarence standing on the porch, watching us. His presence didn't immediately register as significant. As soon as we got back to the house, Clarence called me into the back room.As soon as I entered the room, he immediately hit me a few times and I yelled for him to get off me. As he was hitting me, I fell to the floor and that's when he got on top of me and continued to hit me until his sisters ran into the room. His oldest sister who I will call Meisha hit him and started cursing at him and telling him to leave me alone, so he did. Once we were separated his sisters asked me what happened. I told them that as he was hitting me, he mentioned me flirting with the guy his sister was talking to in his face and saying " I guess that's the man you want to be with" I told him in the middle of him hitting me that I wasn't even talking to him only his sister was. His sister

Toya told him the same thing once we were separated. That day he apologized to me and told me that he would never hit me again, but he did. I was in an abusive relationship with him for two years. I remember one late night an anonymous person called my mom and told her that Clarence had been beating me. Once my mother asked me about it, I lied. I told her that it wasn't true. The call happened because Clarence had busted my nose at the fair that night. After all, I went into the haunted house with one of his male first cousins since he didn't want to, and his cousin asked me to ride with him. I honestly didn't think it was an issue because it was his family. Some of my male cousins even confronted Clarence and threatened to put their hands on him if they found out it was true, and I continued to lie to everyone and say he wasn't hitting me. My dad even told him that he would kill him if he found out it was true once word got back to him and of course, I still lied to him as well.

The relationship ended when I moved to North Carolina with my father for one school semester. Clarence and I were still dating even though it was long distance until one of my male cousins wrote me a letter and told me that Clarence had been cheating on me with a girl who was supposed to be my friend and was my neighbor when I lived with my mother.Clarence was also beating her and worse than he did me. He gave her black eyes which he never left bruises on me. I returned to Alabama for my senior year of high school to graduate alongside the friends I started with in kindergarten. Clarence kept begging me back once he found out I had returned to Alabama. He would call me several times a day and night since I never changed my phone number. He would leave me messages threatening to commit suicide if I didn't get back with him and he even threatened to pay some girls to jump on me because I wouldn't get back with him, but I never did. God just happened to have me meet the girls he promised to pay to jump on me. The two girls came to my house one day with one of my female cousins on my dad's side of the family. When I told them my name, they asked me if I used to date Clarence and I told them I did and that's when they told me that he told them he would pay them to jump on me. The girls and I found out we were cousins and we have been close ever since that day and still close now. God works in mysterious ways. I stood up to him after that and that's when he knew I wasn't that fragile girl anymore and he left me alone eventually. Don't get me wrong I always fought him back and I even cut him one time with a razor blade when he would beat me. The only time I didn't fight back was the very first time he hit me. *"You don't have to see the whole staircase, just to take the first step." ~ Martin Luther King Jr~* I was in a total of three abusive relationships in my past but I'm only going to speak on two of them. My last abusive relationship was fifteen years ago so that was a long time ago. I was in this relationship for five years and I was abused twice in this relationship. The police got called twice in this relationship, but he was only arrested once and that's because the first time I called the police he didn't physically hit me, and the police just talked to us both. He was arrested the last time he put his hands on me. The male officer put my ex in his place since I was pregnant at the time. I'm not going to pretend that I was always innocent because I wasn't, and I even did things to him like throwing things at him, but I never physically put my hands on him. The reason I did those things was because he kept disrespecting me by flirting with girls on social media and then blaming it on him trying to be a rapper and having to entertain the women so they would support the rap career that he never even had. The very first time he hit me was right after we came from church, and I was pregnant with my son. To be honest, I can't remember what the argument was about, but I do remember I started crying in the car and he reached over while he was driving. I was sitting in the passenger seat, and he hit me across my face and told me to shut up. I remember telling him he didn't own me or tell me what to do. The only reason I didn't hit him back was because I was pregnant, and I didn't want to lose my baby. I remember we went into the store, and we were still arguing and people in the store were looking at us and he yelled and told them to mind their business. He didn't hit me again until after my son was born. He relocated to California shortly afterward for a year. The last time he hit me was following an outing with my mom to the casino. While he was at the casino, I took the opportunity to go through one of his old phones. He had just purchased a new one after spending the past year living in California with his dad. As I sifted through his messages and contact list, I saw all these girls' names in his contacts with VIPs beside their name and I even read text messages between him and a girl that were inappropriate for someone who was in a relationship. I called him over the phone and started cursing him out and I threatened to call some of the girls, which angered him. I never called any of the girls, but I just wanted to see how he would react, and by his reaction that let me know all I needed to know. I told him when he got back, he needed to get his belongings and leave but he could come the next day and watch our son while I went to work since that was our routine being that he was unemployed. He didn't come home that night like I asked but the next morning he came over. Not to watch our son like I thought but to get his belongings. Our son was two years old at this time and was lying in his bed asleep. I told him I needed to go to work, and he knew that. I said you can stay here like I told you last night with our son but once I get off you need to leave. He told me that he wasn't going to keep our son and that I could figure it out and he said "F" my job. While he was packing his clothes, I started walking down the stairs to get in my car to leave for work because I knew he wouldn't leave our son by himself, so I just said I'm going to leave. He heard me walking down the stairs and he ran down the stairs, grabbed me by my hair, and started dragging me up these metal stairs by my hair. I never saw him that angry before and he didn't seem like himself. His eyes were bloodshot red, and I thought I saw Satan for a minute. I honestly think he was high off something, and it wasn't weed. That was the first time and the only time that I feared him. I remember screaming and asking him to let me go as he was dragging me by my hair up the stairs. Once he got me to the top of the stairs, he dragged me into the house and hit me a few times and then he let me go. Once he let me go, I jumped from the top stairs to the bottom of the staircase. These were not short stairs either; they were long, narrow, and metal. I can't believe I landed and didn't break a bone in my body. I felt like I had to fight for my life because I honestly thought he was going to kill me. I ran to one of my neighbor's houses. I started beating as hard and loud as I could and as I was doing so, he was running down the stairs chasing me, and he punched a hole in my neighbor's screen door trying to get to me. As soon as he got ready to grab me my female neighbor opened the door, and she immediately shoved him and started hitting him and she told me to get in her house and I called the police. Once he knew I was calling the police he ran upstairs, grabbed our son and took off in the car. His mother called me and told me that she had my son and begged me to drop the charges after he went and turned himself in at the police station. She even tried to use the woman-to-woman and mother-to-mother mess on me to get me to drop the charges, but what angered me was when she said, "he has bruises too" and I told her that she was a liar and that I didn't even put my hands on him. After that day I knew I could no longer be with him or be with an abusive man because I didn't want my son to grow up thinking it was okay to hit women and I didn't want him to grow up in an abusive household the way I did. My son showed me what unconditional love was and I knew it was not being someone's punching bag. I never went to the police station to drop the charges, nor did I attend the three court hearings. I only did that because I didn't want him to have a record and mess him up from having a job and that's only because my dad talked me out of it after he spoke to my ex's mother. My dad said, "Clarence will not be able to provide for you and your son if he can't get a job because that will stay on his record." If I knew what I know now I would have attended all of the court hearings. I never would have listened to my father's advice. My sister tried to convince me to go to court and I wish I would have listened to her. That was a lesson that I had to learn and one of those lessons is that *"LOVE SHOULDN'T HURT"* If you are in an abusive relationship and don't know how to get out, please call the

National Domestic Violence Hotline at 1-800-799-SAFE (7233)

or you can even text BEGIN/START to 88788. If you are in an

abusive relationship or have been and are still struggling

silently join a support group and talk to someone that you trust

such as a relative or friend. I just want you to know that you

are NOT ALONE and STRONGER than you may think.

www.ingramcontent.com/pod-product-compliance
Lightning Source LLC
LaVergne TN
LVHW022324080426
835508LV00013BA/1312